RN MINOR WAR VESSELS IN FOCUS

Lt Cdr Ben Warlow RN

EDITOR'S NOTES

Most Naval Histories concentrate on major actions in which Admirals commanded Fleets comprising battleships, aircraft carriers, cruisers and flotillas of destroyers; where Flotillas, Squadrons and Escort Groups comprising destroyers, frigates and corvettes escorted the ocean convoys; and when submarines traversed the Seven Seas seeking enemy shipping and gathering intelligence. Although these actions changed the course of wars, throughout there were many naval operations conducted, normally away from the glare of publicity, but of vital importance, by a myriad of (usually) smaller craft. It is hard to describe in a few words what ships these were, the types being so diverse. These craft flourished during wars, when the need for their services was greatest, dwindling to virtually nothing in times of peace, when every penny of the Naval (Defence) Budget has to be scrutinised a hundred times over before being spent. Similarly, just as these craft tended to be improvised based on the two factors, availability and (urgent) need, so their crews were mainly drawn from "hostilities only" personnel, who came forward in large numbers in Britain's hour of need.

Some of these minor war vessels formed Coastal Forces, which comprised motor gunboats, motor torpedo boats, motor anti-submarine boats, motor launches and patrol boats. Most of these craft were designed and built specifically for their war role. Others are not so simple to define, often being merchant vessels which became available and which were converted to a military role. Paramount amongst these were trawlers, which were taken up in their hundreds and used for a variety of tasks: minesweeping, patrol duties and anti-submarine work. Along with these came drifters and yachts to supplement the meagre forces available. There were also larger escort vessels built to specifications which allowed for rapid production by shipyards which were unused to warship construction. As each war progressed, there arose specialist requirements. Minesweeping, essential to keep the trade flowing and without which all the efforts to move convoys safely would be brought to nought, became a major task. This volume in the FOCUS series has omitted these minesweeping forces, which are sufficiently large to warrant a separate volume (to be published later). In the Second World War amphibious assaults developed into a major section of naval operations. Lessons were learnt with each operation, resulting in requirements for specialist craft, which were built in large numbers at short notice. These vessels ranged from large personnel carriers, small gun and rocket carrying craft - supplementing the monitors which had been developed in the Great War; to small canoes (for the Combined Operations Pilotage Parties who carried out essential surveys right under the enemy's noses months before an assault). It is a measure of the size of the Navy's involvement in combined operations that by June 1944 some 63,000 officers and men were employed on beach duties and manning landing craft and a further 18,000 officers and men manned the landing ships. In all 113,000 were involved in Combined Operations.

There were also many other tasks to be fulfilled which called for specialist vessels. Surveying the waters through which operations were to be conducted became even more critical as charts had to be updated to show wrecks, and new charts were required for areas not usually travelled in the quiet days of peace. Meanwhile, each harbour required its share of small patrol craft and boom defence and net vessels to protect it against enemy action, and also small craft to run the messages and carry stores between ships and shore. On the offensive side, small craft were developed to take the war to enemy harbours. These included midget submarines, special MTBs and even canoes.

In this volume I have tried to show the wide variety of the minor war vessels of the 20th Century. However, the subject is so great that each section or period in time could take its own volume (as is the case with mine warfare vessels). In searching for photographs I have sometimes sacrificed quality because of the interest of a particular photograph. Both for photographs and information I have been greatly assisted by Geoffrey Hudson (the Coastal Forces Historian) whom, it is to be hoped, will one day soon produce his own work depicting MTBs and MGBs using his great collection of photographs, supplemented with descriptions using his encyclopaedic knowledge of these vessels.

Ben Warlow
Burnham on Crouch
April 2001

HMS JASEUR

HMS JASEUR was a typical Torpedo Gunboat at the end of the 19th Century. Of the 810 ton Alarm Class, she was launched in 1892. She had a speed of just over 19 knots, and was armed with two 4.7-inch guns and carried three tubes to launch the then new weapon- torpedoes. She was sold in 1905. Though outdated by the introduction of the faster torpedo boat destroyers using the new turbine engines, some of the class survived longer to be used as minesweepers or submarine depot ships in the First World War. (World Ship Photo Library)

CMB 95E
CMB 95E was one of a class of 71 such vessels. The first Coastal Motor Boats were completed in 1916 and were used in a raid on Zeebrugge. Their potential was soon realised and developed. CMB 95E completed in September 1919. She was of the 55 ft. class, which could carry one or two 18-inch torpedoes launched over the stern, and depth charges. She had Thornycroft Y12 engines giving her a speed of 41 knots and was armed with a single torpedo trough aft. She became Target CC in December 1925. She was transported to Hong Kong in March 1934, where she was damaged beyond repair and disposed of in January 1937. (Geoffrey Hudson Collection)

ML 307

Some 580 motor launches were built by the Electric Boat Co. in America and by Canadian Vickers in Canada during the First World War. ML 307 was built in Canada. Of 37 tons, these wooden craft were armed with a single 3-pounder gun, and had two petrol engines developing 440 hp, giving them a speed of 19 knots. They were involved in many actions including the Ostend and Zeebrugge raids. (Author's Collection)

HMS AURICULA

The AURICULA was a Flower Class sloop of the Anchusa group. She was a "convoy type" sloop, built to a basic tramp ship design, but with a finer bow and stern. Her decks could either be canvassed in or left open to change her appearance and she operated as a Q-ship under the name HEMPSEED. She was sold in February 1923. (Author's Collection)

HMS GENERAL WOLFE

The monitor GENERAL WOLFE was built in 1915. She carried a twin 12-inch gun forward, and aft she mounted a single 18-inch gun that had come from the battlecruiser FURIOUS. The after gun was mounted so that it always pointed to starboard. The massive armament reflected the importance attached to the support the Navy could (and did) give to the Army in their land battles in Europe in the First World War. She was broken up in 1923. (Author's Collection)

HMS MINERVA

The minelayer MINERVA had been built as the monitor M33, completed in June 1915 by Harland and Wolff with machinery by Workman Clark. Of 535 tons, she was armed with two 6-inch and one 6-pounder guns, and she served at the Dardanelles, in the Aegean and White Sea. Post war she was converted to a minelayer and was named in 1925 when she was a tender to HMS VERNON at Portsmouth. During the Second World War she was a hulk, and was in use as a workshop. She survived and has been the subject of preservation work. Currently (2000) on display in her monitor guise at Portsmouth Naval Base. (Author's Colection)

HMS ROBIN

The Gunboat ROBIN was built by Yarrow in 1934. Typical of the river gunboats designed for work on the Yangtze, she was armed with a 3.7-inch gun, which can be seen above her bridge. She also had a 6-pounder and machine guns. She was based on Hong Kong for her whole career and was bombed when the Japanese attacked the Colony in December 1941. She was finally scuttled there on Christmas Day to prevent her falling into enemy hands. (G. Pulham)

HMS KITTIWAKE

The KITTIWAKE was a Kingfisher Class patrol sloop, later rated as corvette. Of 530 tons, she was built by Thornycroft and completed in April 1937. Her task was coastal convoy escort duties, being armed with a 4-inch gun forward and a multiple machine gun aft, together with depth charge throwers and rails. Powered by geared turbines, she had a speed of 20 knots. She was mined in September 1939 and badly damaged, repairs taking over a year. She was employed off the East Coast throughout the war. She was sold in September 1946 for mercantile use. (Crown Copyright)

HMS GARDENIA

In 1939 the Navy was desperately short of escort vessels, and an emergency programme of building was instigated. GARDENIA was one of the first of the small, handy 925 ton Flower class corvettes of which 280 were ordered. They carried a single 4-inch gun and depth charges. GARDENIA is seen here with her short forecastle and mast forward of her bridge, with external degaussing coils on her hull. Completed in May 1940 at Renfrew, she helped in the withdrawal of troops from France, and then undertook convoy escort duty. She was an escort to convoy HG 76, when the carrier AUDACITY was lost, but 5 U-boats were sunk. Later modified with a long forecastle and extra armament, she was lost in a collision with the trawler FLUELLEN off Oran on 9 November 1942. (Crown Copyright)

MTB 03

MTB 03 was one of the early British Power Boat type of MTBs, completed on 24 August 1936. Three Flotillas of these craft were the only MTBs serving with the Royal Navy at the outbreak of war. They were good seaboats, one Flotilla taking passage to Malta across the Bay of Biscay. Of 18 tons, she carried machine guns and two 18-inch torpedoes (in troughs) which were launched through ports in her stern using gravity and quick acceleration of the boat during the launch. She was capable of 33 knots, and achieved over 35 knots when light. She was disarmed and used as a local motor boat in 1940 and became a controlled target vessel in 1942. She was dismantled for the recovery of useable material in late 1944. (Author's Collection)

MTB 49

Built by Thornycroft, MTB 49 was completed in April 1941. On her first passage to sea she ran aground opposite the Houses of Parliament. She was powered by 4 Thornycroft petrol engines which gave her a maximum speed of 29 knots, with a continuous speed of 26 knots. She was armed with two 21-inch torpedo tubes. She paid off in December 1942 and became the War Office target towing vessel MEGGIDO in February 1943. (Geoffrey Hudson Collection)

MTB 18

MTB 18 was a 33-knot British Power Boat vessel, completed in March 1939 and armed with two 18-inch torpedoes with dropping gear aft (only one set can be seen here, the other being replaced by depth charges). She was a good seaboat but had a light hull, which required much repair. She was seen here, with MTBs 15 and 16 astern, off Felixstowe in February 1940, with her hull painted black. She lost her bow ramming a German minesweeper off the Dutch Coast in August 1940. She was used for target towing as CT 10 in 1942 and was disposed of in 1944. (Geoffrey Hudson Collection)

MGB 8

MGB 8, ex Motor Anti-Submarine Boat 8, was completed by the British Power Boat Co. in May 1940 and was powered by two Napier Sealion petrol engines giving her a speed of 23 knots. She had a hard chine hull, and was armed with a Rolls Royce 2-pounder gun aft and a twin 0.5-inch machine gun. This photograph was taken in May 1942 off Dover. She paid off in September 1944 being no longer seaworthy and was sold in 1947. (Geoffrey Hudson Collection)

MTB 23

MTB 23 was built by Vospers and was powered by three Isotta-Fraschini petrol engines giving her a speed of 42 knots. This photograph was taken in the summer of 1939 when she was on torpedo firing trials, and was carrying extra deck mounted fuel tanks. Armed with two 21-inch torpedo tubes, she was sold to the Royal Romanian Navy in 1939 and renamed VIJELIA. Her design proved the basis for all wartime Vosper MTBs. (Geoffrey Hudson Collection)

MGB 60

MGB 60 was a British Power Boat hard chine boat powered by three Isotta-Fraschini petrol engines and was capable of 40 knots. She had been ordered as an MA/SB for the French Navy, was taken over by Admiralty and later redesignated an MGB. She paid off in August 1944, and was then allocated for control and towing duties. Post war she was used as a house-boat, and in 1998 came under the control of the Coastal Forces Heritage Trust and taken to Lowestoft Harbour heritage area. (Geoffrey Hudson Collection)

MTB 70

MTB 70 was a Vosper 70-ft boat. She was being built for the Royal Hellenic Navy (as T3) and was acquired by the Royal Navy in June 1940. She had two engines instead of the designed three, so was restricted to 27 knots. She was armed with 0.5-inch machine guns on her centreline replacing two 0.303 guns sited on each side, and two 21-inch torpedo tubes. She helped evacuate troops from Le Havre in 1940 and sank an enemy trawler in the Dover Strait in October 1940. She was later used for target towing. (G. Pulham)

MTB 74

MTB 74 was completed in December 1941. Built by Vospers, she replaced the first MTB 74 which was bombed on the stocks. She was specially converted with torpedo tubes on her forecastle to carry Mark 10 depth charges to attack the SCHARNHORST and GNEISENAU then lying in Brest Harbour- but they sailed in February 1942 before the plan could be put into action. She was lost in March 1942 during the St. Nazaire raid when she attacked the Old Entrance to the basins successfully and then was sunk rescuing survivors on her way out of the harbour. (Geoffrey Hudson Collection)

MTB 97

MTB 97 was completed in September 1942. These 72.5-ft Vosper craft were designed by Cdr (E) P du Cane Royal Navy. They had a third rudder to improve manoeuvrability with their three Packard engines. Armed with machine guns, two 21-inch torpedo -tubes and depth charges, they were capable of 40 knots. She was badly damaged in a collision with MTB 89 in October 1942, and was paid off in November 1944. A year later she was sunk as a target off Malta. (Author's Collection)

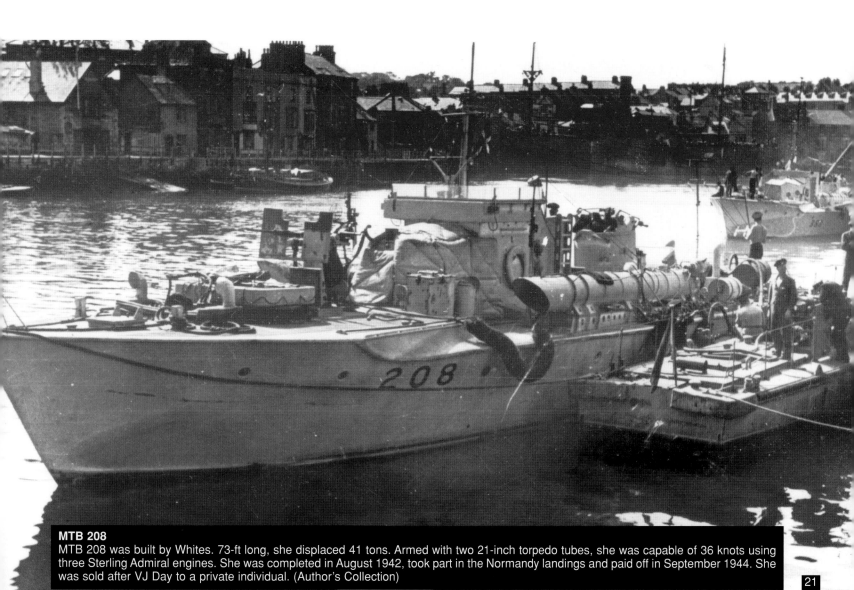

MTB 208
MTB 208 was built by Whites. 73-ft long, she displaced 41 tons. Armed with two 21-inch torpedo tubes, she was capable of 36 knots using three Sterling Admiral engines. She was completed in August 1942, took part in the Normandy landings and paid off in September 1944. She was sold after VJ Day to a private individual. (Author's Collection)

MTB 224

MTB 224 was a Vosper 72.5 foot MTB built at Renfrew. She was completed in April 1942 and powered by three Packard engines, giving her a top speed of 38.9 knots She took part in minelaying operations, attacks against enemy shipping off the Nore, and the Normandy landings. Her gunnery armament varied through her career. She is seen here with her sister boat 244, both with Oerlikons forward, off Shotley. Her main offensive weapons were her two 21-inch torpedo tubes. She was paid off in January 1945 and sold to a private individual by 1949. (Author's Collection)

MTB 263

MTB 263 was built by The Electric Boat Co (ELCO), Bayonne, New Jersey. 70 ft long, she was powered by three Packard engines giving her a speed of 44-45 knots, and was armed with two 21-inch torpedo tubes, two twin 0.5-inch Brownings sited amidships and two twin 0.303-inch Lewis guns forward. She was the US Navy's PT 14 and commissioned in the RN in February 1942. She arrived at Alexandria in April 1942 to serve in the Mediterranean. After an accident in Kos in September 1944 she was reduced to a training role. She was returned to the US in March 1946 at Alexandria. (Geoffrey Hudson Collection)

MTB 315

MTB 315 was built by ELCO, Bayonne, New Jersey and completed in March 1942. She was transferred to the Royal Navy on lease lend and arrived at Alexandria in June 1942. 77 ft long (7 ft longer than earlier ELCO boats) and powered by three Packard engines, she had self sealing fuel tanks. She was armed with two 21-inch torpedo tubes, a 20-mm gun aft, twin 0.5-inch machine guns in power operated turrets amidships and Brownings on her foredeck and also carried 2 depth charges. She served in the Mediterranean and Aegean, and was photographed here at Casteloriso. She was returned to the United States Navy on 10 September 1945. (Crown Copyright)

MGB 115

MGB 115 was a 71.75-ft British Power Boat vessel of 37 tons, with three Packard engines giving her a speed of 42 knots. She was armed with a 2-pounder gun, two 20-mm guns, machine guns and two depth charges. This photograph was taken just after her completion in January 1943. In September 1943 she was converted to a motor torpedo boat and renumbered 434. She was lost in action with R-boats off Le Havre on 9 July 1944. (Geoffrey Hudson Collection)

MTB 209

MTB 209 was built by Whites of Cowes to a Vosper design and completed in September 1942. Her hull was hard chine, of double diagonal mahogany, with a bonded wooden deck. She had Sterling Admiral engines which were 2 tons heavier than the engines for which she was designed, affecting her trim and performance. Photographed here on builder's trials in August 1942, she took part in the Normandy landings and was later listed for disposal in December 1944. (Geoffrey Hudson Collection)

MTB 426

MTB 426 was built by Whites, to their own hull design with a flush deck and light scantlings, and fitted with three Sterling petrol engines giving her a speed of 39.75 knots. She had a combined gun and torpedo armament, carrying a 6-pounder forward, a twin Oerlikon aft and two twin 0.303-inch guns and two 18-inch torpedo tubes. She was completed in August 1944, when she joined the Polish Navy as S7. She returned to the RN in October 1945 and was listed for disposal in December 1945, being sold in 1950. (Geoffrey Hudson Collection)

MTB 290

MTB 290 was a 72.5 ft Vosper boat powered by three Packard petrol engines. Built by Herreshoff Manf. Co., Bristol, Rhode Island, USA, as BPT 32, she was completed in April 1943 and was shipped to the Mediterranean in an LST, being transferred to the RN on Lease Lend. Seen here with a captured Italian Breda gun on her foredeck, she received damage in an air raid on Bari in December 1943. She was laid up at Malta in July 1945 and later destroyed with the consent of the US Authorities. (Geoffrey Hudson Collection)

MTB 422

MTB 422 was built by Higgins, New Orleans and was completed in December 1942. Originally being built for transfer to the USSR, she was transferred to the RN when convoys to Russia were suspended in March 1943. Her extra spaciousness, powerful generators, electric cooking, refrigerator and bunks for all the crew were much admired. She carried two 21-inch torpedo tubes, two twin Brownings, a twin Oerlikon and a 40-mm Bofors. She served in the Adriatic and Mediterranean in 1944/45, and was seen here off Leghorn in February 1945. She was returned to the USN in October 1945. (Geoffrey Hudson Collection)

MTB 358

In this wartime photograph of MTB 358 the censor has deleted her (special type of) radar and radio aerials. She was a Vosper 72.5-ft MTB built by Harland and Wolff in Belfast to a Vosper design, completing in November 1943. In this view it can be seen how every square inch of deck space was utilised, and how cramped conditions were on the bridge. She took part in the Normandy landings (note the white star Allied identification mark on her foredeck) and in December 1944 she was allocated to the High Speed Target Service for target towing. She paid off in May 1945 and was listed for disposal in July 1946. (Author's Collection)

MTB 521

This broadside view of MTB 521 shows her fitted with two 18-inch torpedo tubes, though she could be fitted as a Motor Gun Boat when required. British Power Boat built, she was 71ft 9 inches long and powered by three Packard engines giving her a speed of 39 knots. She was armed with a 6-pounder gun forward and twin 20mm guns aft, and with two 18-inch torpedo tubes. She survived the war and served in the post war Navy as a Radio Control Target Boat before being sold in 1958. (Crown Copyright)

MTB 530

MTB 530 is in the foreground of this photograph of three Vosper MTBs at speed in 1948. She was completed in August 1946 and was the larger (74.5 ft long) version of the Vosper boats. She was renumbered 1030 in 1949 and was lost in a collision with MTB 1032 (see page 48) on 28 March 1952, thirty miles off the Hook of Holland during a NATO exercise. (C. Booth)

ML 100

Motor Launch 100 was the first of the Fairmile A Motor Launches, of which 12 were built. Their design was based on the pre war Fishery Protection Boat VAILA. 110 ft long, she was propelled by three Hall-Scott Defender petrol engines giving her a speed of 25 knots. She was completed in May 1940 and almost her first task was to assist in the Dunkirk evacuation. Her original task was anti-submarine patrols, for which she could carry 12 depth charges. Later she was converted for minelaying, with her funnel removed (as seen here) carrying 9 moored or six ground mines. She was armed with a 3-pounder gun forward. She took part in the Normandy landings and was paid off in March 1945, and sold in October 1947. (World Ship Photo Library)

ML 105

ML 105 was a Fairmile A launch, which was converted to a minelayer in 1942. Of prefabricated construction, and with a hard chine hull, she was powered by three Hall Scott Defender engines giving her a speed of 25 knots. She was armed with a 3-pounder gun aft, two single 0.303-inch guns, a Holman projector and 12 depth charges. She was completed in July 1940, when this photograph was taken, and served in the Nore area on anti-E-boat and minelaying operations, and was involved in the Normandy landings. She was sold in May 1946. (Geoffrey Hudson Collection)

ML 268

ML 268 was one of the many Fairmile B motor launches completed. The first was ordered on 22 September 1939. Many of these vessels were built in the UK and abroad, and served in many Navies. They were very flexible in their tasks, and their armament reflected their role. Strips of metal were fitted on their decks while they were being built which allowed different weapons to be bolted on craft easily. She was built by the Dorset Yacht Co Ltd at Hamworthy, completing in July 1941. She was armed with a 3-pounder, 2 Oerlikons and 4 Lewis guns. She was lent to the Free French Navy in January 1942. In March 1942 she took part in the St. Nazaire Raid, carrying troops for the Old Entrance. She was hit and set on fire as she turned towards her target and blew up before she reached the shore. (Geoffrey Hudson Collection)

MI 172

ML 172 was a Fairmile B Motor Launch completed in March 1941 by Francis Curtis, Looe. Originally armed with a 3-pounder, a Holman Projector, machine guns and depth charges, she was fitted with two 21-inch torpedo tubes from ex-American destroyers at Gibraltar in January 1942. She was photographed here operating out of Gibraltar in 1944. She later took part in minesweeping operations in the Adriatic. These craft were 112 ft long and were powered by two Hall-Scott Defender petrol engines giving them a speed of 20 knots. Originally these vessels were to have had three engines, but the supply position restricted this, and instead 50 percent more boats were built each fitted with just two engines. (C. Booth)

ML 878

ML 878 was another Fairmile B launch, built in Egypt and completed on 23 March 1945. This photograph was taken in the Bitter Lakes as she was on her way to the East Indies. She was the gunboat version of these craft. 48 were so built for the Arakan Theatre. As a gunboat she had a 6-pounder forward, a twin Oerlikon on the engine room hatch and a 2-pounder pom-pom aft, with 2 rocket flare launchers. She was fitted with Type 268 radar. She had a short career, operating from Bombay and in December 1945 she was laid up at Trincomalee before being dismantled for recovery of spares in February 1946. (Geoffrey Hudson Collection)

MGB 312

MGB 312 was a Fairmile C vessel powered by three Hall Scott petrol engines giving her a speed of 26.5 knots. She was armed with two 2-pounders and machine guns. Completed in June 1941 by Woodnutt on the Isle of Wight, she took German radar back to UK from the Bruneval raid, took part in the Dieppe raid and Normandy Landings. This photograph was taken in 1944 when she had a power operated pom-pom forward, a high angle pom-pom, a single Oerlikon and four barrelled 0.303-inch Vickers machine guns (known as "deck sweepers" - unique to the 1st CF Flotilla). She paid off in October 1944 and was listed for disposal in October 1945. These vessels were a modified version of the Fairmile A type. (Geoffrey Hudson Collection)

MGB 606

MGB 606 was an early Fairmile D completed by Wallasea Bay Yacht Co. without torpedo tubes in July 1942. This photograph was taken during her work up off Weymouth. These early vessels had no "scallops" in the hull to help torpedoes to clear the tubes, so when fitted as an MTB in 1943 her 18-inch torpedo tubes had to be mounted on high supports. Her original armament comprised a 2-pounder pom-pom forward, twin Oerlikon aft, two twin 0.5 Vickers and two twin 0.303 Vickers guns and two depth charges. She was later fitted with a 6-pounder gun. She was sunk in action off the Dutch coast after being repeatedly hit and set on fire on the night of 3 November 1943. Attempts to tow her failed. (Geoffrey Hudson Collection)

MTB 651

MTB 651 was a Fairmile D vessel completed by Toughs of Teddington in January 1943. She was completed without torpedo tubes and had 18-inch tubes fitted later. She was photographed here off Ancona in May 1945 with an additional twin Oerlikon above the engine room and a USN radar set. She, with MTB 640 and 670 helped sink the Italian Submarine FLUTTO North of Sicily in July 1943. She served in the Adriatic in 1945 until September when she was listed for disposal. (Geoffrey Hudson Collection)

MTB 724

MTB 724 was a later Fairmile D vessel completed in September 1943 by the Wallasea Bay Yacht Co. Ltd.. She was photographed off Weymouth with four 18-inch torpedo tubes and the usual gun armament of a 2-pounder pom-pom, two twin 0.5 inch Vickers, two twin 0.303-inch Vickers, a twin Oerlikon and a 6-pounder aft and two depth charges. She took part in the Normandy landings and in September 1944 was in an action off Ostend in which 3 E-boats were destroyed. She was lent to the Norwich Sea Cadets in December 1945 and sold in July 1954. (Geoffrey Hudson Collection)

MTB 5008

MTB 5008 was of the modified Fairmile D design, and was fitted with two 21-inch torpedo tubes. She has a 6-pounder forward and aft, an Oerlikon abaft the bridge and machine guns on each quarter of the bridge. Built at Burnham on Crouch, this photograph was taken during her trials on the Crouch. She was not completed until June 1945, having been converted for operations in northern waters. Post war she was armed with two short 4.5-inch guns, one forward and one aft. She was sold in July 1956. (Author's Collection)

MGB 506/GAY VIKING

MGB 506 was building by Camper and Nicholsons for the Turkish Navy but taken over by the Admiralty. She completed in August 1943 and two months later transferred to the Ministry of War Transport for use as a mercantile vessel for anti-blockade runs to Sweden, and was named GAY VIKING. For that operation she served under the Red Ensign and was operated by the Ellerman and Wilson Line. 117 ft long and powered by three Davey Paxman diesels, giving her 26 knots, and was armed with two twin Oerlikons and two twin and one quadruple 0.303 Vickers guns. She was lost in collision with a sister ship, HOPEWELL, in the Skaggerak on 5 February 1945. (Geoffrey Hudson Collection)

ML 1029

ML 1029 was a Harbour Defence Motor Launch of 72 ft, powered by two Glennifer DC8 diesels giving her a speed of 11.5 knots. She was built by McGruer and completed in September 1940 and was used for training at Portland and later at Ardrishaig. She carried a 2-pounder forward, 0.303-inch Lewis aft, a Holman Projector and 8 depth charges. She was listed for disposal in 1946. These were round bilge vessels and many were built in the UK and abroad. (Geoffrey Hudson Collection)

ML 1384

ML 1384 was also an HDML, built by R A Newman of Hamworthy. She was powered by Gardner 823 diesels and commissioned in August 1943. She originally carried a 2-pounder forward, an Oerlikon aft and two twin 0.303-inch guns. She was shipped to the Levant in December 1943 and was based at Alexandria and also Massawa. She operated off the West Coast of Italy in 1945. This photograph was taken in February 1946 at Malta, when she had an Oerlikon forward and a minesweeping winch aft for an Oropesa Mk V Sweep. She paid off at Malta in September 1946. (Geoffrey Hudson Collection)

SGB 8/HMS GREY WOLF

SGB 8 was completed by William Denny in April 1942. She was named GREY WOLF in June 1943. These powerful vessels were steam propelled, but it was found that their boilers were vulnerable to gunfire, and the extra armour required to counter this reduced their speed from 35 to 30 knots. Her armament comprised (from forward to aft) a single Oerlikon, a Holman Projector, a pom-pom, two twin 0.5-inch Vickers, 6 twin 0.303-inch Vickers, two 21-inch torpedo tubes, a pom-pom, a 3-inch, and a single Oerlikon - a total of 21 gun barrels. She saw action in the Channel, including the Dieppe Raid and in the Seine Bay in June 1944. She was sold in February 1948. (Geoffrey Hudson Collection)

MTB 537/CT 8045

MTB 537 was built by Vospers and completed in December 1945 as a controlled target boat (CT 45). She was later renumbered CT 8045 and served until 1957, being sold in October 1958. Designed for 40 knots and to carry a 6-pounder, other light guns and two torpedo tubes (a sister boat was MTB 523 - see rear cover), in this task she was unarmed. A wide variety of MTBs/MGBs filled the CT role as they became unfit for operational patrols, but when MTB 537 was completing in 1945 the Navy could afford the luxury of a new vessel filling this role. She was fitted with a petrol driven winch on her stern for towing. (Author's Collection)

P1032

P1032 (ex MTB 532) was a Vosper built MTB in 1946. 73 ft long she was capable of 40 knots and was armed with a single 4.5-inch gun forward, machine guns, Oerlikons and two 18-inch torpedo tubes. In March 1950 off the Hook of Holland she collided with MTB 1030 (see page 32), which sank. She was used as a dumb power lighter at HMS DILIGENCE in the 1950s and was sold in April 1957. (Author's Collection)

P5518

P5518, ex MTB 518, ex MGB 518, was built by Camper and Nicholson and completed in July 1946. She displaced 115 tons, was 117 ft long, and was powered by 3 Packard engines giving her a speed of 31 knots, and carried four 18-inch torpedo tubes. Her original gunnery armament comprised two 6-pounders and six 20-mm. The forward 6-pounder was later replaced by a 4.5-inch gun, but subsequently most of her guns were removed and she carried a derrick and two surf boats for operations with the Special Boat Service. This class had an increased beam and a knuckle running two feet below deck level to reduce their "wetness". In all they were very handsome vessels. She served after the war, being sold in March 1956. (Author's Collection)

P5212
P5212 was an ex German E-boat, ex S212, taken over by the Royal Navy for trials and experiments after the war. She had been built in 1943 by Lurssen, Vegesack and was powered by Mercedes Benz diesel engines giving her a speed of 38 knots. The different torpedo tubes arrangement from RN vessels is clearly visible in this photograph. She was sold in August 1957. (Author's Collection)

P2009

P2009 was originally MGB 509, built by Camper and Nicholson. Ordered for the Turkish Navy, she was taken over by the Admiralty in February 1941, launched in April 1943 and formed part of the Naval Intelligence Division Flotilla employed on clandestine operations. 117 ft long, she had three Paxman diesel engines and a speed of 31 knots. After the war (in 1948) she was given a Gatric gas turbine engine for trials, the first naval vessel powered by a gas turbine to go to sea. The gas turbine drove her centre shaft, whilst she had two V12 Packard engines on the other two shafts. She was listed for disposal in December 1951, and was sold in 1954 to be broken up. (G. Pulham)

HMS GREY GOOSE

The Steam Gun Boat GREY GOOSE (sister to GREY WOLF - see Page 46) was retained after the war and her engines replaced by two experimental Rolls-Royce RM 60 marine gas turbines driving Rotol controllable pitch propellers. These trials proved very successful and led the way to future patrol craft, and later larger warships, being given this form of propulsion. She was sold in December 1957. (Author's Collection)

HMY GLEN STRATHALLAN

The desperate need for ships in 1939 was reflected in the types of craft requisitioned. Among these was the yacht GLEN STRATHALLAN, built in 1928 and of 330 tons, slightly smaller than the average trawler, she had a speed of 12 knots. She was hired as an anti-submarine yacht from September 1939 to November 1945. She is photographed at Holyhead in May 1944, where she was employed on radar trials. (Crown Copyright)

HMT SIR KAY

One of the Round Table class, the smallest of the Naval trawlers at 440 tons. Built by Hall Russell of Aberdeen based on their 1932 STAR OF ORKNEY. She had an "A" bracket on her bows for an acoustic sweep and a deckhouse forward containing 2 diesel generators to power an LL sweep, a cable that carried electrical impulses to detonate magnetic mines. The sweep had to be manhandled as there was no power winch. She took part in the Normandy operation and in 1945 was at Ostend before being laid up in July 1945. She became the mercantile THE STAR OF THE NORTH. (Geoffrey Hudson Collection)

HMT KINGSTON AMBER

The KINGSTON AMBER was requisitioned for anti-submarine duties in September 1939. This small, 467 ton, vessel was armed with a 4-inch gun forward, a twin 0.5-inch machine gun aft and two 0.303-inch guns. She had a speed of 12 knots. She operated around the United Kingdom for the first few years of the war, and in 1942 undertook convoy rescue duties before being based on the Faeroes. In September 1943 she was sent to the Azores, and operated from there from January 1944 until March 1945. She paid off in August 1945 and was returned to trade in February 1946. (Geoffrey Hudson Collection)

HMS ELLESMERE

HMS ELLESMERE was a Lake Class whaler, ex-KOS XXIV built by Smith's Dock in 1939. Of 560 tons, she was armed with a 12-pounder gun forward (replaced by a 4-inch gun later) and had a 20-mm gun aft as well as machine guns. She was one of the craft purchased in 1939 to increase the number of escort vessels. These whalers were very good seaboats, and could maintain escort duties when destroyers had to shelter from bad weather. She took part in the 1940 Norwegian campaign and escorted an assault convoy to Normandy. She was sunk by U-1203 on 24 February 1945 in the Channel whilst escorting a convoy. It was U-1203's only operational patrol of the war, and ELLESMERE was her only victim. (Geoffrey Hudson Collection)

HMT EGILSAY

The EGILSAY was launched by Cook, Welton and Gemmell of Beverley in February 1942, and was armed with a 12-pounder gun forward. She was lent to the Italian Navy in 1946 and sold to them later. She became their RD 306. (Geoffrey Hudson Collection)

HMT COLDSTREAMER

The trawler COLDSTREAMER was of the 750 ton Military Class, launched by Cook, Welton and Gemmell on 10 December 1942. She was completed in April 1943 and was fitted out for anti-submarine duties and armed with a 4-inch gun forward and four Oerlikons. She was used on ocean escort duties in the Western Approaches and crossed the Atlantic many times during the war, calling at St. John's, Newfoundland and at Iceland. She was sold to a Hull fishing company in April 1946 and was renamed ESQUIMAUX. (Geoffrey Hudson Collection)

HMT FARNE

The FARNE was an Isles Class trawler launched on 22 April 1943. She was completed as a danlayer to operate with the Fleet minesweepers, and as such did not carry the usual 12-pounder gun forward. Whilst operating with the Fleet minesweeper LARNE off Harwich she was known as FARNDAN to avoid confusion. She was with the 7th Flotilla sweeping for D-Day. Sold into merchant service in 1947 and lost in December 1948. (Geoffrey Hudson Collection)

HMS BARITONE

BARITONE was a Bar Class boom defence vessel, one of a very large class that were capable of ocean voyages and which were deployed world wide on mainly unsung but important duties in support of the main fleet. These vessels had a bow lifting capacity of 70 tons, and had a rounded stern to ease the handling of hawsers and kedge anchor. She was built by Philip and Son of Dartmouth and launched on 3 March 1945. She was sold in 1958, though others of the class served for even longer. Of 750 tons, she was armed with a single 12-pounder gun which was mounted abaft her funnel, and had two Lewis guns. Her coal-fired engines could develop 850 SHP giving her a top speed of 11.75 knots. (D. Scoble)

LCP(M)

These craft were Landing Craft Personnel (Medium), known as "Cobles" or "Viking Craft". They were designed for beaches that were too rocky or rugged for Landing Craft Assault (see page 62). They could carry 20 fully armed troops at 7.5 knots, being powered by single Scripps Ford V8 petrol engines. They required a crew of 3. These craft were photographed taking part in the Cheduba Landings in the East Indies in January 1945. (Author's Collection)

LCA

These Landing Craft Assault were also seen taking part in the Cheduba Landings in the Far East. They were sturdy boats 38 ft 9 inches long and capable of 10.5 knots. They could carry 36 troops and had a crew of 4. Their ramp forward made for easier landing during the assault and the coxswain had a small lightly armoured conning position forward. (Author's Collection)

MLC 17

MLC17 was an early Landing Craft Mechanised, built by Philip and Son of Dartmouth. She could carry a 16-ton tank or 6 jeeps or 100 troops, and was light enough to be hoisted into a larger ship for passage to the assault area. She was powered by twin Gill jets and fitted with rotating nozzles to improve manoeuvrability. She was abandoned in June 1940 during the evacuation of Dunkirk. (D. Scoble)

LCT (4) 537

LCT (4) 537 was built in 1942 and was powered by two Paxman diesel engines and capable of 9.5 knots. She could carry 6 x 40-ton tanks or 9 x 30-ton tanks or 13 loaded 3 ton lorries or 350 tons of cargo. They could land tanks in up to 3 feet of water on beaches with a gradient of 1 in 150 or less. These vessels were also used for tending nets etc. LCT 537 was damaged in October 1943, and was paid off at Naples in January 1944, when she became Yard Craft No 3001, being used as a dumb lighter there until being written off in May 1953. (Author's Collection)

LCS(L) Mk1 201

The LCS(L) Mk 1 was for use against tanks ashore, and was armed with a 4-inch smoke mortar, a 2-pounder and Besa gun in a Daimler turret, and four machine guns. These craft were of Thornycroft design and wooden construction vessels powered by two Gray diesels with a speed of 10.75 knots. LCS 201, ex-Heavy Support Craft 41, was sunk in collision with LCS 202 on 1 September 1943 in the English Channel. (Author's Collection)

LCS(L)(2) 257

LCS(L) Mk 2 257 was a Fairmile H type large support craft, commissioned in June 1943. She was armed with a 4-inch smoke mortar in a well forward, and a 6-pounder gun in a turret as well as with a twin 20-mm and machine guns, to provide artillery support to landing craft. Powered by two Hall Scott Defender engines she was capable of 14.5 knots and her role was to support LCTs during an assault in an anti-tank role. She took part in the Normandy landings and was sold to the Warsash Yacht Co in December 1945. (Geoffrey Hudson Collection)

LCF (3) 4
LCF(3) 4 was a Landing Craft Flak Mark III, designed to operate with other landing craft during an assault and provide anti-aircraft cover. A converted LCT of 485 tons (550 full load), she was powered by two Paxman diesel engines and had a speed of 11 knots. She was armed with eight single 2-pounders mounted en echelon in her tank deck and four 20-mm forward and aft. She was damaged during the Dieppe raid in August 1942. She paid off to reserve at Messina in July 1945 and transferred to the Italian Navy in March 1946. (Geoffrey Hudson Collection)

LCS(M) 33

These 10.5 ton craft were constructed of wood and metal and partially armoured. She was armed with a turret containing two 0.5-inch Vickers guns (behind and above the coxswain's head), and two 0.303-inch Lewis guns and a 4-inch smoke mortar. She was propelled by a Scripps V8 petrol engine. Eight such craft were built to support small landing craft during assault operations. She became Naval Auxiliary Boat 86 in February 1945. (Author's Collection)

LBK 1

Landing Barge Kitchen No 1 was a self propelled barge of 150 tons fitted with two petrol engines to drive her at 6 knots. She was originally a Landing Barge (LBV 158) and was converted to an LBK between February and May 1944. She carried stores in her hold, and had a galley to feed crews of landing craft. She was capable of feeding 900 troops for one week, baking bread, and had a 10 ton water tank. She was used in the Normandy landings (Gold Beach -where she was known as "Mickey's Fish and Chip Bar"), and later with Force T at Ostend. Her role was an essential, if unsung, part of an amphibious operation prior to the establishment of catering facilities ashore. She became Yard Craft 3029 as a cooking lighter at Portsmouth Dockyard in 1945. She was lent to the Israeli Navy from 1966-68, and was finally sold on 3 April 1970. (Geoffrey Hudson Collection)

HMS HIGHWAY

The first experiments with Landing Ships Tank (which were to carry tanks on longer sea voyages than was convenient with LCTs) were not successful. Thus Landing Ships Docks were built to carry the LCTs (laden with tanks) in their docks to the landing area, where they could be undocked to make their way to the beaches. The LSTs did, eventually, prove successful, but many LPD's were built. HIGHWAY, seen here with 4 Harbour Defence Motor Launches in her dock, was built at Newport News (where these HDMLs were also built) and launched in July 1943. Of 4270 tons, she was capable of 16 knots. Four of the class served in the Royal Navy, and 13 with the USN. She was returned to the USN in April 1946. Some of her class were still with the USN in the 1970s. They proved very useful for providing docking for maintenance and repair services in the amphibious operating areas. (Crown Copyright)

LST 3019/VAAGSO

L3019 was a Landing Ship Tank completed in December 1944 by Swan Hunter. These vessels were designed to carry tanks and heavy vehicles on long sea voyages direct to the beaches for an assault. The British built LSTs were steam powered, whilst those built in the USA were diesel driven. They could carry 15 x 40 ton tanks or 27 x 25 ton tanks, or 14 x 3 ton lorries and 168 troops. L3019 took part in the relief of Norway and was later named VAAGSO. She was placed in care and maintenance in September 1946 and plans to convert her to an AA firing ship in 1949 were cancelled. She was broken up in December 1959. Some of these craft survive even today, despite having been built with a short life expectation in view of their hazardous role. (Crown Copyright)

LCVP

Post war developments based on the considerable wartime experience of amphibious operations led to the introduction of the larger assault ships, which were equipped with Landing Craft Vehicle-Personnel (LCVP). This example was carried by the Commando Carrier HMS BULWARK in the 1970s, and shows how they could be hoisted and lowered, and had the coxswain in a protective area aft. Note the radar reflector mounted on the LCVP in the background to allow for "blind" direction of the craft from the parent ship. These 43 feet long craft could carry 35 fully equipped troops or a mix of vehicles, stores and men. (Crown Copyright)

LCM (9) 706

LCM (9) 706 was a further post war development of amphibious operations. The LPDs FEARLESS and INTREPID were designed to carry four of these craft in their docks to land stores, vehicles and men in any amphibious operation. They could carry two battle tanks or 100 tons of vehicles. This craft, operating from the INTREPID can be seen landing a beach recovery vehicle. The engines of these craft are right aft and specially designed to leave the cargo deck clear, and they are fitted with Kort nozzles for beaching and precise steering ahead or astern. (Crown Copyright)

HM SM X23

Not all operations were overt, and the epitome of the silent approach was the midget submarine. X23, photographed here approaching the Headquarters Ship LARGS at Normandy on D-Day, was typical. She was unofficially named XIPHIAS (Swordfish). She had helped mark the approaches for the assault forces to aid their navigation. These craft were also used in reconnaissance of beaches, and for attacks on enemy shipping, famously the attack on the German battleship TIRPITZ. X23, built by Markham & Co. Ltd., Chesterfield, was completed on 12 December 1943. She was of 27 tons and had a crew of 4. Her main armament comprised two charges, each of 4 tons, slung on each side. She was broken up in 1945. A sister ship, X24, is preserved at the Submarine Museum at Gosport. (Author's Collection)

HM SM XE 8

The midget submarine XE8 is photographed here alongside a Motor Fishing Vessel, which was used as a support vessel. The submarine had the unofficial name EXPUNGER or EXUBERANT- it is understood the name moved with the Commanding Officer- whilst the MFV was unofficially named EXCORT. XE8 was built by Broadbent, Huddersfield and was designed for Far Eastern operations and so given better habitability. She displaced 30 tons and carried two 4-ton charges. She was capable of 6.6 knots on the surface and just over 6 knots submerged, and carried a crew of 4 or 5 men. In the Far East these vessels cut communications cables and carried out a successful attack on Singapore Harbour, sinking the Japanese cruiser TAKAO. She was scrapped in 1952. (Author's Collection)

HMS SHACKLETON

The SHACKLETON started her career as the Halcyon class minesweeper SHARPSHOOTER, being built at Devonport in 1936. During the war she took part in the Dunkirk evacuation, where she was damaged in a collision; Russian Convoys, where she rammed and sank U-655 in March 1942; and operations in the Mediterranean, where she was damaged by a torpedo. She was converted for survey duties by Silley Weir, Blackwall, in 1946 and served in the Singapore area in 1946-1947 before returning to UK waters. Her name was changed in 1953. She was broken up in November 1965. (Author's Collection)

HMS MEDA

The MEDA was a Harbour Defence Motor Launch converted for inshore survey work. Originally number 1301, and built in Bideford in 1943, she took part in the Salerno landing in September 1943 and was in action at Elba (Op Brassard) in June 1944. She was powered by Gardner diesels and had a speed of between 11 and 12.5 knots. In 1949 she relieved the GULNARE on South Coast Survey operations. She was sold in May 1966. (Author's Collection)

HMS FAWN

HMS FAWN was designed for overseas survey duties, operating with a sister ship. She was launched in February 1968 by Brooke Marine, Lowestoft, and was powered by 4 Lister Blackstone diesel engines, giving her a speed of 15 knots. She had a range of 4,500 miles at 11.5 knots. She carried a 6.8 tonne survey motor boat for shallow water surveys. She paid off in 1991 and was sold for mercantile use, being renamed RED FULMAR and providing off shore support for oil exploration off West Africa and in the China Sea. (Crown Copyright)

HMS ECHO

HMS ECHO was one of three inshore survey vessels of 165 tons built on hulls similar to contemporary inshore minesweepers. She was launched by Whites of Cowes in May 1957. Her role was to survey coastal waters and harbours around the British Isles. She was sold to the Marine Society in August 1986 and renamed the EARL OF ROMSEY and is used as a training ship. (Crown Copyright)

HMMTB GAY DRAGOON

GAY DRAGOON was a post-war petrol driven MTB which could be fitted as an MGB or Minelayer. She was built by J. Taylor of Chertsey in 1953. Here she was fitted as an MTB with two 21-inch torpedo tubes. Designed by Vospers, the hulls were of entirely wood construction and capable of 40 knots. She was sold in December 1961. (Crown Copyright)

HMMTB DARK ROVER

DARK ROVER (ex-DARK CAVALIER) was another of the composite construction MTB/MGB Dark Class vessels, built by Vospers and completed in October 1956. She is seen here fitted as an MTB, with a 40-mm gun forward and two 21-inch torpedo tubes, and depth charges. The Napier Deltic engines fitted in these craft had the best power/weight ratio then achieved in a marine diesel engine. She was sold in 1966 and became an Italian Customs launch. (Author's Collection)

HMMGB BOLD PATHFINDER

BOLD PATHFINDER was completed in July 1953 by Vospers. With a round bilge, she was of light alloy construction and had twin funnels. She displaced 133 tons and was powered by two gas turbines, with two diesels for cruising, driving four propellers. She had a top speed of 43 knots and is seen here with her MGB profile of two single 4.5-inch guns and a 40-mm gun. She was sold in May 1962. (Crown Copyright)

HM FPB BRAVE BORDERER

The Fast Patrol Boat BRAVE BORDERER was built by Vospers Ltd., Portsmouth, in 1958-60. She had a composite wood and metal construction and a hard chine hull form. With three Proteus gas turbines developing 10,500 horse power, she had a speed in excess of 50 knots and was seen here armed with two single 40-mm guns and four 21-inch torpedoes. Originally the Brave Class were to be fitted with a new 3.3 inch gun, but trials of the gun in FPB BOLD PIONEER were not a success. BRAVE BORDERER was sold in 1985. (Crown Copyright)

HMS SHALFORD

SHALFORD was a Seaward Defence Boat of 120 tons. The first of her class, she was unusual in being fitted with a Squid anti-submarine mortar aft, the only one of her class so fitted. She was completed by Yarrow in 1955, and was powered by 2 Paxman diesel engines giving her a speed of 18 knots. She also had a third (Foden) engine driving her centre shaft for cruising. She was sold in October 1967 at Singapore for breaking up. (Maritime Photo Library)

SANS HAERLEM

HAERLEM was one of three Ford Class Seaward Defence Boats specially built for the South African Navy by Vospers. She was launched on 18 June 1958 and was fitted with roll damping fins developed by Vospers. She had distinctive twin funnels, was armed with a 40-mm gun forward and carried depth charges. Later in her career she was used as a survey vessel. On 30 November 1987 she was sunk as an artificial reef off Port Elizabeth. Many of this class transferred to, or were built for, foreign and Commonwealth Navies. (G. Pulham)

HMFTB SCIMITAR

Three Fast Training Boats were built by Vosper-Thornycroft in 1969/70. They had 100-ft long hulls of glued laminated wood construction. Developed from the Brave Class Fast Patrol Boats, they were powered by two Proteus gas turbines, with two Foden engines for cruising. They had a maximum speed of 40 knots and were used off Portland to give the Fleet experience in dealing with the threat posed by fast patrol boats. They could be fitted with a third gas turbine engine and with light missiles if required. SCIMITAR, seen here operating with Rigid Raiding craft, was completed in July 1970 and served for a period in Hong Kong. She was sold in 1983, becoming the Greek AQUILON. (Maritime Photo Library)

HMFPB TENACITY

TENACITY was a Vosper-Thornycroft private venture, launched in February 1969. She was powered by three Proteus gas turbines giving her a speed of 40 knots, but she also had two Maybach diesels on wing shafts for cruising at 16 knots. Designed to carry two twin Sea Killer surface to surface missiles and a twin 35-mm gun, she was commissioned into the Royal Navy on 17 February 1973, re-armed and used for exercises and fishery protection. She was listed for disposal in 1980 and was sold in 1985. (Crown Copyright)

HMS SPEEDY
The Hydrofoil SPEEDY was built by Boeing Marine at Seattle and commissioned at Portsmouth on 14 June 1980. She was a hard chine hydrofoil of all aluminium construction and could travel at 43 knots on her foils. She was sold in September 1984 and became the SPEEDY PRINCESS. (Crown Copyright)

HOVERCRAFT BHN-7

This 33 ton (light) hovercraft (Wellington BHN-7 type) was one of several used in trials by the Navy, and was the first hover warship, joining the Inter services Trials Unit at Lee-on-Solent in April 1970. She underwent cold weather trials in Swedish waters in 1972. Possible uses for such craft were for minesweeping, as missile armed fast patrol craft or as amphibious assault craft. Her single Rolls Royce Proteus Gas Turbine could drive her at 60 knots, and she could carry 60 troops or be fitted with 7 tons of armament. She was deleted in 1985. (Crown Copyright)

HMS PROTECTOR

PROTECTOR was launched by Yarrow in 1936 as a netlayer designed to lay special barrages to protect the fleet. This made her very beamy. She was badly damaged by torpedo bombers during the war, and was repaired in India. Completion of repairs was delayed until 1945 as two sets of the special turbines she required for her powerful engines were lost on passage from the UK. In 1954-55 she was converted to an ice patrol ship by Devonport Dockyard. A twin 4-inch gun was mounted forward and a flight deck and hangar fitted aft. She served for many years as the Falklands Islands patrol vessel, before being broken up in 1970. (Author's Collection)

HMS YARNTON

The YARNTON was one of the Ton Class coastal minesweepers, some of which were built as minehunters. They had a double mahogany hull and were constructed of aluminium alloy and other materials with the lowest possible magnetic signature. She was completed in January 1957 by Wm. Pickersgill & Son, Sunderland, and in 1971 was converted at Hong Kong to a patrol craft, with a 40-mm gun forward and one aft, and two pedestals for 7.62-mm machine guns. Five of the class were converted, a second, MONKTON is visible in the background of this photograph, and these vessels then operated from Hong Kong until relieved by the Peacock Class patrol vessels. YARNTON was sold in 1986. (Crown Copyright)

HMS ANGLESEY

The Island class offshore patrol vessels were built for the Royal Navy by Hall Russell, Aberdeen. They were designed to protect British interests in the North Sea, oil installations and fishing grounds. Five were ordered in 1975, and two further vessels in 1979. The two later vessels were built with significantly enlarged bilge keels to suppress motion in heavy seas, a feature which was retrofitted in the first five. Of 925 tons displacement, they are powered by diesel engines giving them a speed of 16.5 knots, and were armed with a single 40-mm gun, later replaced by a 20-mm or 30-mm gun. They also carry a semi-rigid craft for boarding. With a range of 7,000 miles at 12 knots, these ships have clocked up much sea time in their careers. ANGLESEY was launched in October 1970 and was of the second batch. She was still serving in 2001. (Crown Copyright)

HMS LEEDS CASTLE

The LEEDS CASTLE was laid down as a speculative venture as an offshore patrol vessel by Hall Russell of Aberdeen, and purchased by the Royal Navy whilst building. She was launched in October 1980 and was armed with a 40-mm gun forward (later replaced by a B-Marc 30-mm) and has a flight deck aft and can refuel Sea King or Lynx helicopters. Fitted with two Ruston 12RKC diesel engines giving a range of 10,000 miles at 10 knots, they have a maximum speed of 20 knots. They carry two Sea Rider high speed craft for boarding and can be used as minelayers. Both vessels of this class served in the Falkland War, and afterwards shared the task of Falklands Islands Patrol Vessel between them. She was still serving in 2000. (Crown Copyright)

HMS PEACOCK

Five Peacock Class Patrol Boats were ordered in 1981 to replace the aging Ton Class patrol vessels (ex minesweepers) for duty in Hong Kong to back up the local police force. The Hong Kong Government met 75% of their building and maintenance costs. Built by Hall Russell of Aberdeen, these 662 tonne craft had two Crossley Pielstick diesel engines giving them a speed of 25 knots. They were armed with a 76-mm Oto Melara gun forward and had pedestals for 4 GPMGs and carried two Sea Rider Boarding craft. Their decks aft were clear to carry up to 100 people. Two were sold to Ireland in 1988, and three to the Philippines in 1997. PEACOCK, which was launched by Hall Russell, Aberdeen in December 1982, was one of those sold to the Philippines. She left Hong Kong on 30 June 1997 and was renamed EMILIO JACINTO when handed over to the Philippine Navy on 1 August 1997. (Crown Copyright)

HMS CYGNET

Bird Class Patrol Boats were similar to the RAF Seal Class vessels. 120 ft long, they were powered by two Paxman diesel engines giving them a speed of 21 knots (19.5-kts maximum continuous). They were used for fishery protection duties and for training, whilst two served as guard ships at Gibraltar, and were built to carry a 40-mm gun and two 7.62 machine guns. CYGNET, which had been completed in July 1976 by Richard Dunstan, was fitted with an enclosed bridge later in her career. After fishery protection duties, she was employed in the Northern Ireland squadron. She was sold in February 1986. The class was replaced by the River Class minesweepers in 1993. (Crown Copyright)

INDEX